THIS BOOK BELONGS TO:

DAVID HARTLEY

(from Mia, Father's Day 2012)

D1736261

Published by Tate Publishing & Enterprises, LLC
127 E. Trade Center Terrace | Mustang, Oklahoma 73064 USA
1.888.361.9473 | www.tatepublishing.com

Tate Publishing is committed to excellence in the publishing industry. The company reflects the philosophy established by the founders, based on Psalm 68:11,
"The Lord gave the word and great was the company of those who published it."

Book design copyright © 2008 by Tate Publishing, LLC. All rights reserved.
Cover design & Interior design by Eddie Russell
Illustration by Jason Hutton

Published in the United States of America

ISBN: 978-1-60604-622-7
1. Juvenile Non-Fiction: Animals: Birds: 1-7
2. Education: General
08.09.30

"WHAT CHEER, WHAT CHEER,"

Says the Cardinal!

TATE PUBLISHING & Enterprises

Written by Martha Scott

Illustrated by Jason Hutton

In Memory of my beloved friend and mentor

MRS. ERMA COLLEY MCKENZIE

She taught me the wonders of bird watching, a truly humbling adventure.

Northern Cardinal

My brilliant red body, bill, and crest
Make me easy to see in flight and in the nest.

Colorful too, my mate rejoices.
Singing joyfully year-round, we have
great voices.

My color and song have brought me fame.
The church cardinals' red robes gave me my
bright name.

I became the first state bird to know.
Then I was picked by six other states that
followed.

TIDBITS

Relatives: Grosbeaks and Buntings

Song: what-cheer-what-cheer and sweet-sweet-sweet

Eggs: 3—4 pale green eggs with red-brown spots

Incubation: 11—13 days

Food: seeds and insects

EASTERN PHOEBE

Here I sit merrily on this branch.
I am often seen doing my tail-wagging dance.

Perched near my moss-lined nest by the creek
I may dart out quickly to catch bugs in my beak.

I'm a tame gray songbird with a dark head.
On his leg my ancestor wore a silver thread.

He was important in history,
First banded bird in North America's scenery.

TIDBITS

Relatives: Flycatchers

Song: fee-bee

Eggs: 4—5 white eggs

Incubation: 15—16 days

Food: flying insects and berries

INDIGO BUNTING

A splash of brilliant blue sailing by,
My feathers are black, not blue.
I promise; no lie.

I'm not really what I seem to be.
The blue is the way the sunlight reflects off me.

Pesky insects and wildflower seeds
Are what I love to dine on, so easy to please.

My babies are born from eggs pale blue.
Raised in my nest might be a cowbird
fledgling too.

TIDBITS

Relatives: Cardinals and Grosbeaks

Song: *sweet-sweet-sweet* and *where-where-where-here-here-see-it-see-it*

Eggs: 3–4 pale blue eggs

Incubation: 12–13 days

Food: insects and *wildflower seeds*

BLACK-CAPPED CHICKADEE

I often eat hanging upside down.
I munch bug eggs, seeds, and berries,
all yummy chow.

Other kinds of birds flock around me.
When danger approaches I warn them all to flee.

I'm very curious and quite tame.
I may sit in your hand, and you won't be
the same.

If you stay calm, to you I will come.
My little black-capped body will sit on
your thumb.

TIDBITS

Relatives: Carolina Chickadees and Tufted Titmice

Song: chick-a-dee-dee-dee

Eggs: 6–8 white eggs with brown speckles

Incubation: 12–13 days

Food: insect eggs, seeds, and berries

AMERICAN GOLDFINCH

Wild canary is what I am called.
My sunny, yellow body is a joy to all.

I search the countryside for my lunch.
Thistle seeds are my favorite snack to munch.

I have a deep nest in a small tree.
This nest, so well-made, can hold water easily.

I say, my home is quite a big mess.
My mate and I aren't good housekeepers,
I confess.

TIDBITS

Relatives: Purple Finches, House Finches, and Pine Siskins

Song: per-chick-o-ree

Eggs: 5 bluish-white eggs

Incubation: 12—14 days

Food: insects, wildflower seeds, and sunflower seeds

PURPLE FINCH

My color is more raspberry-red.
A cup of grasses and twigs is my tree nest bed.

My nest is built in green Christmas trees.
My home is really hidden and is hard to see.

I have a strong bill for cracking food.
I feast on seeds, berries, apples, and pecans too.

Sunflower seeds are my tasty treat.
My nestling babies like caterpillars to eat.

TIDBITS

Relatives: American Goldfinches, House Finches, and Pine Siskins

Song: tick

Eggs: 4—5 blue-green eggs

Incubation: 14 days

Food: berries, other fruits, and seeds

WHITE-BREASTED NUTHATCH

The only songbird with this talent,
I walk down trees headfirst with my super
toes bent.

This way I find insects easily.
Peanut butter's good too, if you want to feed me.

A small tree cavity is my home.
I stay with my mate year-round, so I'm not alone.

First called "nuthack" by early settlers,
I can catch a falling nut, ruffling no feathers.

TIDBITS

Relatives: Red-breasted Nuthatches and Brown-headed Nuthatches

Song: yank-yank and to-what-what-what-what

Eggs: 5—6 white eggs

Incubation: 12 days

Food: tree bark insects, tree nuts, berries, and sunflower seeds

DOWNY
WOODPECKER

I drum on trees with my short, sharp bill.
My tongue flicks out, and I eat bugs to my fill.

It's good that my skull is very thick.
The constant hammering doesn't make my
brain sick.

Of all the woodpeckers in the east
I am the most common and also the least.

With both people and birds I am friendly.
I court my mate in the open for all to see.

Tidbits

Relatives: Hairy Woodpeckers, Red-headed Woodpeckers, Pileated Woodpeckers, and Yellow-bellied Sapsuckers

Song: pik

Eggs: 4–5 white eggs

Incubation: 12 days

Food: insect eggs, nuts, and berries

CEDAR WAXWING

I am a bandit with my black mask.
I steal delicious fruit and berries, if you ask.

I like big crowds, a hundred or more.
With so many friends with me, I never feel poor.

We swiftly move in, quick as a flash.
We're looking for food and a birdbath for
a splash.

Together we sit, all on a limb.
We pass food down the line, from me to her
to him.

Tidbits

Relatives: Bohemian Waxwings

Song: sree

Eggs: 4—5 bluish-gray eggs with dark brown spots

Incubation: 12—16 days

Food: insects and berries

EASTERN BLUEBIRD

I'm called the first announcer of spring,
The bluebird of happiness, bringer of
good things.

Humans have saved the birds of my kind
By building us boxes fit for nesting to find.

My mate and I raise two baby broods.
The first brood stays around to bring the
second food.

It's instinctive for them to help out.
Called cooperative brooding, it's great, no doubt!

TIDBITS

Relatives: Robins and Thrushes

Song: tru-al-ly-tru-al-ly and queedle

Eggs: 4–6 pale blue eggs

Incubation: 14 days

Food: insects, berries, and other fruits

BIBLIOGRAPHY

Batt, Al. "Hands Down, Chickadees Are His Favorite." *Birds & Blooms,* January 1999.

Bull, John, and John Farrand, Jr. *National Audubon Society Field Guide to North American Birds: Eastern Region.* New York: Alfred A. Knopf, Inc., 1994.

Gerring, Mary. "Bird Tales: A Beautiful Mess." *Birds & Blooms,* December/January 2007.

Harrison, George. "Bluebirds." *Birds & Blooms,* February/March 2005.

Harrison, George. "Downy Woodpecker." *Birds & Blooms,* December/ January 2007.

Harrison, Hal H. *The Peterson Field Guide Series: A Field Guide to Birds' Nests of the Eastern United States.* Edited by Roger Tory Peterson. Boston: Houghton Mifflin Company, 1975.

Klutz Press. *Everybody's Everywhere Backyard Bird Book.* Palo Alto, CA: Klutz Press, 1992.

Lamb, Heather. "There's Plenty to Sing About for a Northern Cardinal." *Birds & Blooms,* December/January 2003.

Mace, Alice E., ed. *The Birds Around Us.* San Francisco, CA: Ortho Books, 1986.

Weidensaul, Scott. *National Audubon Society First Field Guide: Birds.* New York: Scholastic Inc., 1998.

e|LIVE

listen|imagine|view|experience

AUDIO BOOK DOWNLOAD INCLUDED WITH THIS BOOK!

In your hands you hold a complete digital entertainment package. Besides purchasing the paper version of this book, this book includes a free download of the audio version of this book. Simply use the code listed below when visiting our website. Once downloaded to your computer, you can listen to the book through your computer's speakers, burn it to an audio CD or save the file to your portable music device (such as Apple's popular iPod) and listen on the go!

How to get your free audio book digital download:

1. Visit www.tatepublishing.com and click on the e|LIVE logo on the home page.
2. Enter the following coupon code:
   227d-fb36-a139-f4f9-6993-f41c-4f15-41b3
3. Download the audio book from your e|LIVE digital locker and begin enjoying your new digital entertainment package today!